Neil, Buzz, and Mike
Go to the Moon

Neil, Buzz, and Mike Go to the Moon

Written and illustrated by Richard Hilliard

Boyds Mills Press

Many Years Ago, there were three boys who dreamed of flying. Neil lived in Ohio and loved running through the grass holding a small wooden airplane high over his head. Just like Neil, Buzz and Mike wanted to fly airplanes when they grew up, too.

NEIL ARMSTRONG

Born August 5, 1930, in Wapakoneta, Ohio.

EDUCATION: Bachelor of science degree in aeronautical engineering from Purdue University; master of science degree in aerospace engineering from the University of Southern California.

EDWIN "BUZZ" ALDRIN

Born January 20, 1930, in Montclair, New Jersey.

EDUCATION: Bachelor of science degree from the United States Military Academy at West Point; doctorate of science in astronautics from the Massachusetts Institute of Technology.

MICHAEL COLLINS

Born October 31, 1930, in Rome, Italy.

EDUCATION: Bachelor of science degree from the United States Military Academy at West Point.

Studying hard in school and college, all three later became pilots in the U.S. military. After flying many missions and testing new types of aircraft, they were selected as members of the Astronaut Corps. This was a great honor.

The astronauts were doing things that nobody had ever done before: flying rockets into space and preparing for the day that man would walk on the Moon. The first space missions were called Mercury, and the astronauts flew in tiny one-man capsules.

The goals of Project Mercury were to put a single astronaut in orbit, control the capsule, and guide it safely back to Earth. Also important was the study of the human body in the weightless vacuum of space, which would help make sure that a trip to the Moon was physically possible for future astronauts. The Mercury capsules were only about 9 feet tall and very tight for the astronaut inside. Six different Mercury missions flew from 1961 to 1963.

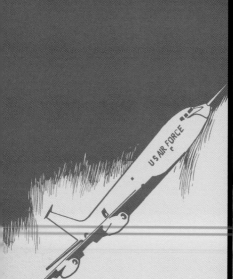

The "Vomit Comet" is a KC-135 four-engine jet transport. By flying almost straight up and then straight down, the plane can simulate weightlessness for the astronauts in the cargo area. During training, the astronauts can practice eating, drinking, and using different kinds of equipment. Each dive of the plane gives the astronauts about one minute of weightless training. Training sessions normally last from one to two hours, with many trips up and down.

Training to go into space was hard work, and not everyone made it. Trainees flew in an airplane that simulated weightlessness. The plane was called the "Vomit Comet" because it made many of the trainees sick. Luckily, Neil, Buzz, and Mike were able to pass this difficult test.

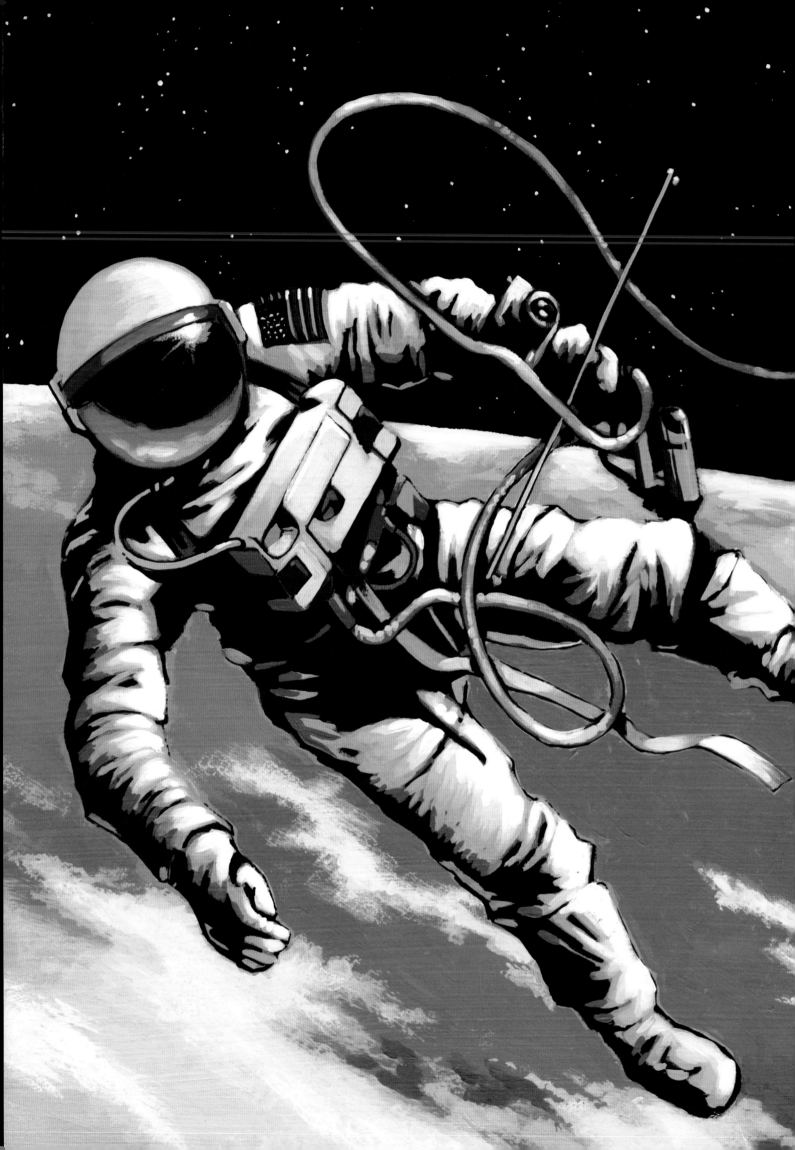

The goals of Project Gemini were to put two astronauts in orbit, control the capsule with precision, and direct the capsule to meet other orbiting equipment. This is called a *rendezvous* and is important when taking multiple spacecraft to the Moon. The capsule was larger and allowed the astronauts to open the doors, or hatches, so they could walk in space and work outside the capsule. Ten different Gemini missions flew from 1965 to 1966.

Along with other astronauts, Neil, Buzz, and Mike were part of the Gemini program, in which they learned how to walk and work in space while flying in a two-man capsule. Buzz even came up with a plan for building and fixing things in orbit, which is not easy because of the lack of gravity.

The goals of Project Apollo were to take a crew of three astronauts to the Moon, land two of them on its surface while one remained in orbit, and return them safely to Earth. The early missions involved testing the new equipment in Earth's orbit, while later excursions headed toward the Moon. Eleven manned Apollo missions flew from 1967 to 1972. Everyone knew the missions would be dangerous, but the crew of *Apollo 1* would make the ultimate sacrifice. Their names were Gus Grissom, Ed White, and Roger Chaffee.

The rockets built to go to the
Moon were called Apollo.
The first test mission ended in
disaster, when a fire ripped
through the capsule and all three
astronauts inside were killed.
Almost two years passed before
the United States was ready to
fly again in safer spacecraft.

After a number of successful test flights, three men orbited the Moon for the first time in *Apollo 8*. It took more than a week to get to the Moon and return home. Confined in their capsule, the astronauts had to eat, sleep, and do everything else that people usually do.

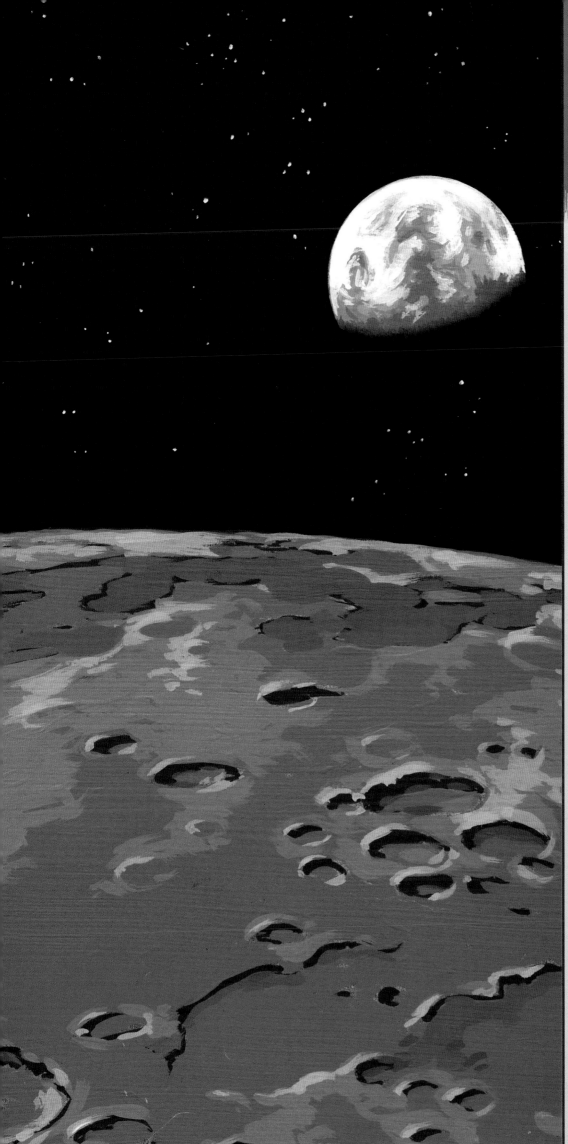

The Moon is our closest neighbor in space, but it is still a long way from Earth. More than 220,000 miles away, the Moon takes about twenty-seven days to orbit Earth. Because the Moon is much smaller than our planet, the gravity is one-sixth of what we experience here. That means that a 180-pound astronaut weighs only 30 pounds on the lunar surface and can jump six times higher. The Moon has many geographic features, including mountains, valleys, and crater-covered plains. The temperature on the surface can be as hot as 250 degrees (Fahrenheit) in the direct sunlight or as cold as -280 degrees (Fahrenheit) in the lunar night.

The time had finally come! The three astronauts chosen to go to the Moon in *Apollo 11* were Neil Armstrong, Buzz Aldrin, and Michael Collins. All of their hard work and determination had brought them to this place in history, and they were ready to go.

One of the largest and most powerful rockets ever built, the Saturn V was 363 feet tall, which is taller than a thirty-six-story building. It had eight main sections, including the Command and Service Module and the Lunar Module. At liftoff, the first stage of the rocket burned more than four million pounds of fuel to escape Earth's gravity. This took the rocket 40 miles above Earth's surface. Then the first stage dropped off, and the second and third stages took over, bringing the crew close to the Moon.

On July 16, 1969, the mighty Saturn V rocket blasted off from Cape Kennedy, Florida, with Neil, Buzz, and Mike on board. The five giant rocket engines shook the ground for miles around as the Saturn V left Earth.

Once in space, only the Command and Service Modules and Lunar Module were needed, as the rest of the empty fuel cells were left behind. Neil, Buzz, and Mike were on their way to the Moon.

Command Module

Service Module

For most of the trip to the Moon and back, the Command Module was home. It was a living room, bedroom, bathroom, and laboratory all in one. Air conditioned and pressure controlled, the module enabled the astronauts to remove their space suits after liftoff and work inside wearing jumpsuits. Attached to the Command Module was the Service Module. It held fuel, water, and oxygen needed for the crew to survive and maneuver in space.

Looking much like a spider, the Lunar Module (LM) was used for only one purpose — landing on the Moon and getting the astronauts back to the Command Module. Made of lightweight materials, the LM did not even have seats for the crew, which saved space and reduced weight. The astronauts piloted the vehicle within the top half of the module. The bottom half held fuel and the main descent engine. That part was left behind on the Moon as the top half ascended to rejoin the Command and Service Module in orbit.

Mike stayed in orbit while Buzz and Neil went into the Lunar Module and started their descent toward the Moon. Nearly running out of fuel, Neil and Buzz found a safe place to land. Neil told everyone back on Earth, "Tranquility Base here. The *Eagle* has landed."

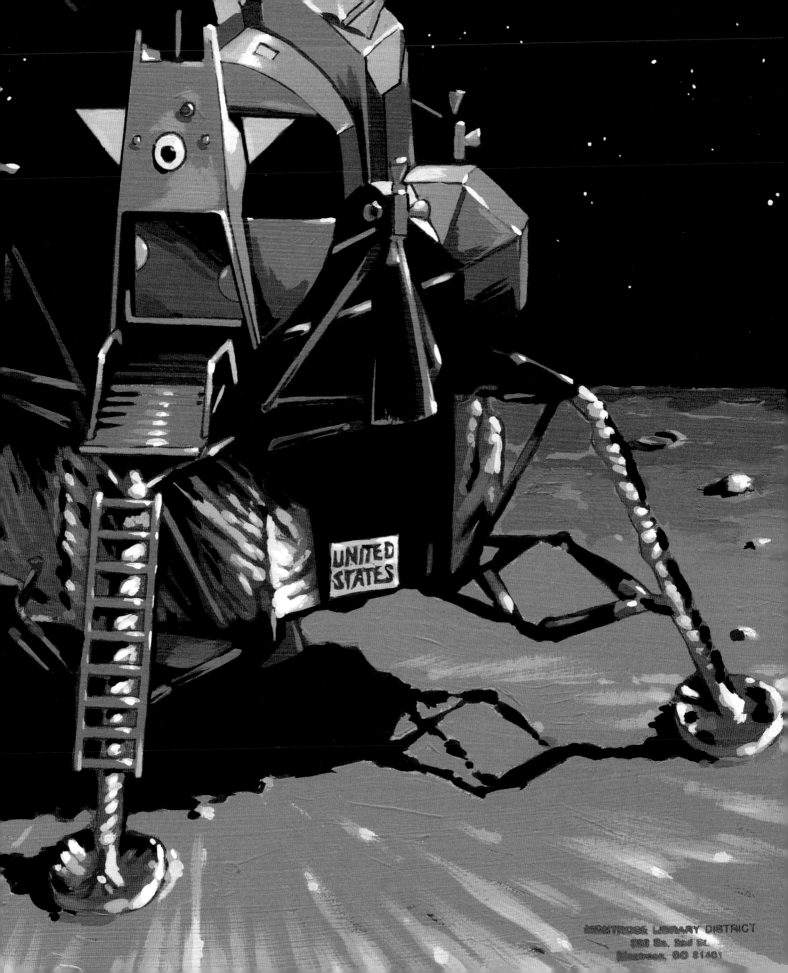

UNITED STATES

the Moon, with Buzz right behind him. The date was
July 20, 1969. They collected many samples of rocks and
dust from the surface to take back to Earth for study.

After exploring the Moon for three hours, Neil and Buzz climbed
into the Lunar Module and flew back to Mike, leaving behind
some equipment and many footprints. These footprints were
evidence of mankind's first steps in the exploration of space.

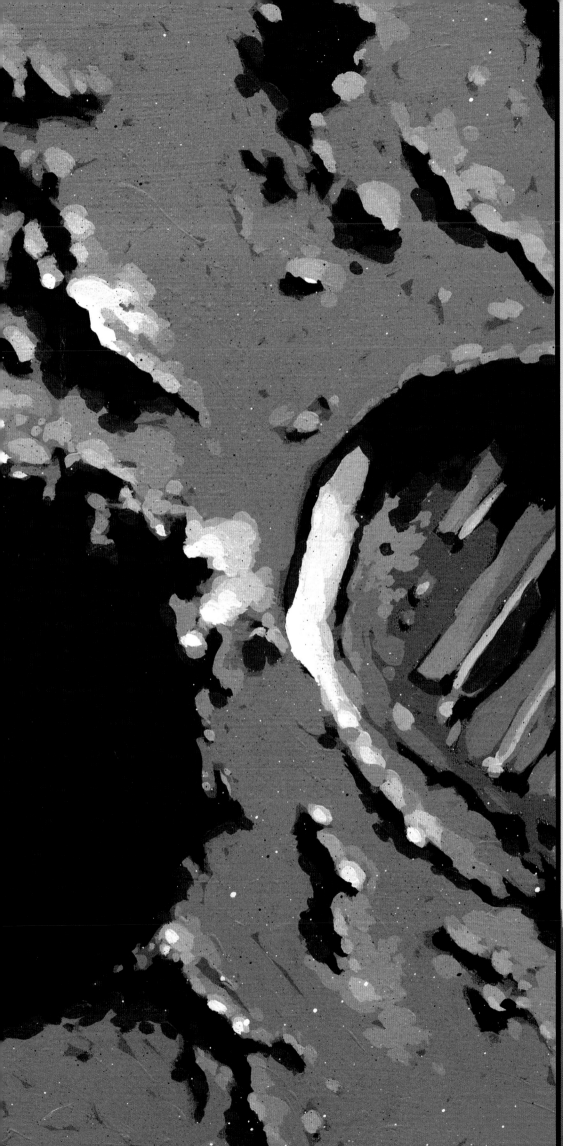

Holding everything an astronaut needed to stay alive in space was the job of the space suit. It kept the temperature of and the pressure on the wearer constant so he could work comfortably. Whether in the cold vacuum of space or the boiling temperature of the sun-baked lunar surface, an astronaut felt no discomfort. The backpack held oxygen, water, and radio equipment for communication with the other astronauts and Mission Control on Earth.

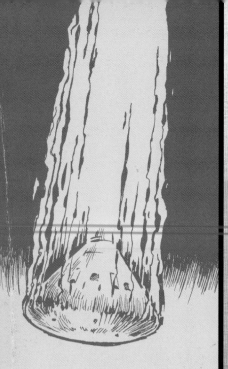

A few days later, the space capsule splashed down in the Pacific Ocean. History had been made, and Neil Armstrong, Buzz Aldrin, and Michael Collins became heroes whose names were known around the world!

Coming back into Earth's atmosphere is dangerous. As the Command Module fell to Earth, heat built up on the capsule's underside, creating a fireball. At top speed, the Command Module fell at more than 24,000 miles per hour. A heat shield protected the module from burning up. As the Command Module neared splashdown, giant parachutes opened. The capsule floated gently down into the water, where waiting helicopters picked up the astronauts. No one knew if there were germs on the Moon that might infect people, so the astronauts had to wear special suits. When they returned to land, they had to live in an airtight house for twenty-one days to make sure they did not get sick or spread any "Moon germs."